Reneé Sunday, M.D.

Sunday Publishing Company
Conyers, Georgia

Sunday Grief M.D. Copyright © 2013 by Renee' Sunday, M.D.

All rights reserved. Printed in the United States of America. No part of this publication may be reproduced, stored in a retrieval system, or transmitted, in any form or by any means electronic, mechanical, photocopying, recording, or otherwise, without the prior written permission of the author except in the case of brief quotations embodied in critical articles and reviews. For information address Sunday Company at the address below.

**Unless otherwise noted, all scripture quotations are taken from the King James Version of the Bible.

Cover by: Donna Osborn Clark at:

CreationsbyDonna@gmail.com

Typesetting and Interior Design by:

Interiorbookdesigns.com

ISBN 978-09890673-0-0

Library of Congress Control Number: 2013905155

Published by:

Sunday Publishing Company

2890 GA Hwy 212 Suite 153

Conyers, Georgia

(205) 249-7451

www.sundaypublishingcompany.com

SUNDAY GRIEF, M.D. SIGNATURE PAGE

MAY GOD BLESS AND KEEP YOU IS MY PRAYER

TO:

_____

FROM:

_____

RENEE' SUNDAY, M.D.

William Sunday, Jr.

"Gentle Giant"

We love you

The Sunday and Williams Family

To My Lord and Savior Jesus Christ, thank You for giving me the gift of writing to empower, inspire, and educate others.

To the Sunday and Williams Family, I express great gratitude and appreciation for your prayers and encouragement.

This book was created to be a powerful resource and support to others when there is a death of loved ones, friends, or associates. The peace of God is the answer.

Acknowledgments

Above all, glory and praise to my Lord and Savior Jesus Christ for all that He has done in my life, and for guiding me throughout the process of completing this work.

God's Plan orchestrates the right people to come into my life at the right time. God's timing is always perfect. Not too early and not too late. Thank you, Lord for allowing me to be in the lineage of the Sunday family.

Special thanks to my family: Mrs. Rosetta and Mr. William Sunday, Sr. Thank God for my earthly angels as parents. To Cassandra, Clifford Sr., Christiana, Clifford Jr., Lashurn, Andria, Amber and Ashley. Thank you for always believing in me, and for always offering me unconditional love.

I would also like to express my sincere gratitude to all of the many people who have had an impact on my life, especially my Birmingham, Atlanta, and Gainesville families for the positive impact and invaluable contributions throughout the years.

I am indebted to many other vessels used by God as pastors, instructors, and mentors, all of whose names I am unable to list here.

~Reviews~

Fantastic book cover fits book perfectly.
"A heartwarmingly poignant book about GOD and Medicine and GOD IN Medicine.
Written by a physician whose commitment to her family and patients is fueled by her commitment to GOD."

Patricia Tarantula Shambaugh, PA
University of Florida, Gainesville, Florida

"This book is concise, easy to read and hard to put down. It contains all the mind-body-spirit information I wish I have known during my early grief.
Most important: Renee' consistently points the reader to God, our true healer."

Sandi Elzinga, author of GriefWalk: Hope Through the Dark Places, a blog for those who have lost a loved one.

Sunday Grief, M.D. is going to be such an encouragement to people who have lost a loved one! I can tell reading it that you poured your heart out and let people know what you went through and how they can receive the comfort, strength and peace that only God can give! I can't say one thing that I would change!

Not only did you tell your story, but you gave ways to help people cope with their grief. That is what will be helpful to many who read it also!

I am so glad that God has been with you and shown himself faithful through such a terrible loss. It becomes such a time of spiritual growth doesn't it?

You are off to a great start to a wonderful ministry!

Dee Huizenga
Author of the blog - Gods Gift's of Hope

"Renee Sunday has written an intensely personal story of how a family can recover from a devastating and sudden loss by relying on their faith. Dr. Sunday's experience as a medical professional adds another layer to the family story as she views the event through the eyes of science as well as faith. I was drawn particularly to the stories of how losing her brother has made Dr. Sunday a better doctor. She and her family are an inspiration to those on the journey of grief.

I know you will bless many through your work!"

Dawn Davis Anderson, M. Div.
Congregational Care Minister and Grief Support Group Leader

"We can always use the Word of God to assist us in our time of bereavement which often leaves us with unhappy and

painful emotions. Dr. Renee' Sunday has experienced family grief in her life and this book will provide practical wisdom and inspiration to console many hearts, souls and minds."
Bishop Willie A. Battles
Bishop of Unity Temple International Fellowship Church
Williston, Florida

"Sunday Grief is both touching and insightful. Renee shares her search for relief from the excruciating pain and loss, the result of the premature death of a loved one. In dealing with the accompanying fear and sorrow, she ultimately finds peace in reconnecting with her Source, God."

Dr. Terry A. Gordon
Author, *No Storm Lasts Forever*
Dr. Gordon shares from personal experience how a so-called tragedy in one's life can actually be a blessing in disguise.

Contents

Foreword ii
Introduction 1
Chapter 1 - The Gentle Giant 3
Chapter 2 - Family 25
Chapter 3 - Emotional Response 29
Chapter 4 - Physical Response 35
Chapter 5 - Spiritual Response 41
Chapter 6 - Transition 49
Chapter 7 - Faith and Anesthesia 61
Chapter 8 - A Mother and Father's Love 69
Chapter 9 - Bringing It All Together 77
About the Author 83
Sunday Publishing Company Journal 85

Yes, God loves us.
God's Love is all around us.

Let not your heart be troubled; ye believe in God, believe also in me. John 14:1

And we know that all things work together for good to them that love God, to them who are the called according to his purpose. Romans 8:28

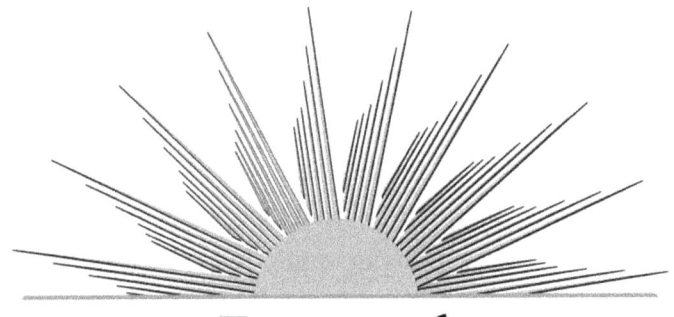

Foreword

The demise, passing away, or loss of a loved one all adds up to one single word "death". It is a word few of us want to deal with. It is a word few of us are prepared to deal with. But it is a word all of us must deal with…one way or another. Death drops one immediately into a myriad of seasons that spell "grief". It's painful, it's awkward, it's "emotional", it's "physical" and it's "spiritual". How does one handle it? How does one get through it? This book that you are holding in your hand will teach you how. Because that's what Dr. Renee' Sunday's book is all about – not just sharing her story, but helping you change the end of your story. As an anesthesiologist in medicine with another sister that is a family practice physician…Renee' reveals immediately that there are some physical circumstances that even "doctors in the family can't change". She skillfully turns your attention to biblical/medical truths that are authenticated by the "physician of physicians", Jesus our Lord and Savior.

When you lose a relative, a friend, a business associate, neighbor or sister/brother in the body of Christ you need to know what, when and how to navigate through the waters of losing a loved one to death. Now I must warn you, if you are not ready to be confronted with truth (truth that sets one free) then you need to put this book down right now! For Renee' Sunday, is one of few persons that dares to tell it like it is. She literally invites you into her personal space…when not many years ago her younger brother died suddenly. Gentle but honest, vulnerable but strong, hurting but healing…she becomes Christ-like. Remember Jesus on the Cross of Calvary…while hurting the most, he was healing the most for "by his stripes we are healed". Dr. Sunday reached out to all of us 'while hurting most' to 'heal' all of us experiencing the painful seasons of grief.

Step by step, Dr. Sunday provides truth wrapped around knowledge, information and wisdom to guide you from 'grieving to grinning' – literally. If she does not address all of your questions and concerns, she gives enough information to inspire your own journey to health and recovery after losing a loved one in death. I salute her for writing this book – all nine chapters; I salute you for reading this book – all of it. You are on your way to a healthy recovery…watch and see!

Dr. Wanda
Author, Minister, Mentor

What questions do you ponder during the healing process of grief? Will you see your loved ones again? How to cope each day through this process?

In this book, Dr. Renee Sunday teaches us how to apply powerful prayer and develop support by seeking God's guidance. With this powerful testimonial, this book will change many lives.

Emotions can be overwhelming in the midst of grief, she describes in her book what she experienced and what steps can be taken to get through when she felt like a raging storm. Oftentimes, we don't realize that physicians experience pain along with adapting in uncomfortable situations in their surroundings. She shows us that God's grace is sufficient no matter who you are. She also shows her strength and Faith by trusting the authority of God.

I found that when I lost "Mattie" the greatest prayer for me was the prayer of patience. God can give us the patience we need to overcome obstacles and challenges. You may sometimes experience anger and even question your faith, but I survived my storm by remembering "Mattie's" words of wisdom and encouragement which gave me strength day to day.

In this amazing testimony, Dr. R. Sunday gives us several examples of ways to handle our loss, most of all, she assures God's love and that He is big enough to handle all questions. "Thank you, Renee Sunday for equipping all of God's people who may be dealing with death or have dealt with sadness in their lives." You have spoken from the perspective of an Individual, Christian, and Physician helping us to see that God can carry us through our difficulties; we must trust Him through our experiences.

God Bless,
Evangelist, Stephanis Battles- Brown

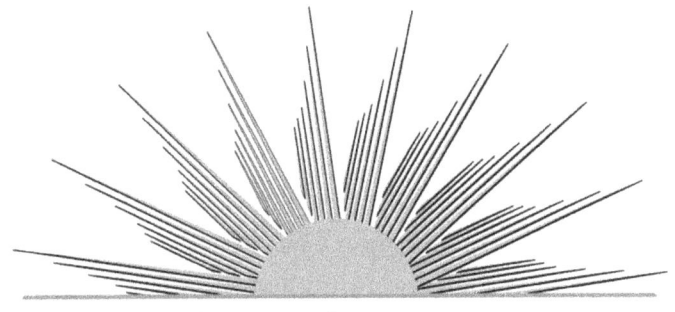

Introduction

There are two occurrences in life that are 100% guaranteed: being born and the other is dying. When a person dies or passes on from Earth, the remaining people (family, friends, and associates) go through the different phases or levels of grief. The grieving process can consist of physical, emotional, and spiritual responses. Your response will not be the same as another person's response. God created all of us in His image. We have different dreams and goals in life. We have different responses to stress and situations. As a medical professional, I experience first-hand how the body functions and performs on a daily basis. God's masterpiece— the human body can sense and respond differently depending if the stimuli are positive or negative. The Word of God is our compass and direction in life. When the Sunday family proceeded through the grieving process ONLY God supplied peace, joy, and a renewed mind in Him. I will share our journey to resting in God's arms. The Word of God will encourage and strengthen us along life's pathway. God is the ONLY refuge when trials and tribulations come. God is the antidote to going through the grieving process. God will comfort and give confidence. Yes, God had already made the way for me and my family to proceed through the grieving process. This book displays my love for my brother, Junior. I will share the process of grief through my eyes of being his sister and an anesthesiologist. God has given me this mission to express wisdom and guidance to inspire others to trust God throughout the grieving process.

"Teaching them to observe everything that I have commanded you, and behold, I am with you all the days (perpetually, uniformly, and on every occasion), to the [very] close and consummation of the age. Amen (so let it be)."

Matthew 28:20* AMP

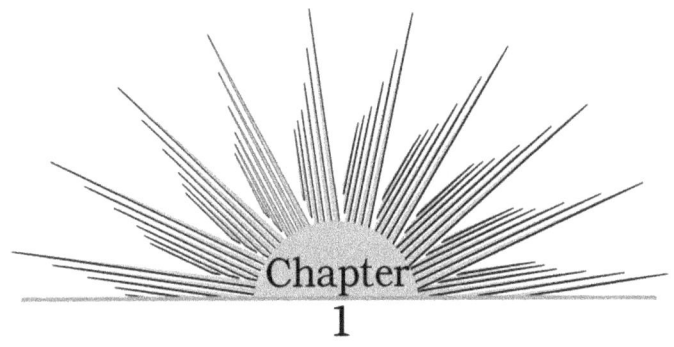

Chapter 1
The Gentle Giant

The glow of the lights surrounding the White House, as I flew by during a crisp and quiet night brought thoughts of joy, love, and laughter. The song "God Bless America" came to mind. A peaceful appreciation of living and progressing toward my destiny in life had led me to a conference in Washington, D.C. I awakened to a beautiful and amazing sunrise with God's comforting presence all around me.

Unfortunately, I wasn't feeling well. My body was tired, and my stomach was queasy. I lay in bed and listened to a gospel program. The message was how God will always make a way, and nothing comes in our life that we cannot handle. I believed this statement. During the conference, I was a student in various classes – I learned a lot of valuable information in the process of continuing my destiny in life. I was assertive and confident, and enjoyed the first day of the event. In the convention hall, my cell phone reception was awful, and I was unable to receive any calls or texts. I didn't think anything of it at the time.

After my short walk back to the hotel, I received a voice mail from my sister-in-law, Lashurn. She said my brother had been taken to the hospital. I quickly contacted my family. At this point, my brother was awake and talking.

My brother, William Sunday, Jr., 37, a college student, had gone back to college and was majoring in psychology after several years of being out of high school. I was proud he had returned to college and felt this was a blessing from God. He was smart in high school, and only needed limited study time, and did well in all of his classes. But he decided to enter the workforce rather than go on to college. Our whole family was happy that, after several years, he was back in school.

He enjoyed being a student again. William – we called him "Junior" – would call me and say, "I like expanding my knowledge and accomplishing one class after another." He also said, "Renee, I know why you and Cassandra reached the mountain top and obtained your dreams in life. When you learn one thing, it escalates to a pyramid of pride and enjoyment." Cassandra is my older sister, and we call her San, short for Sandra. To hear my younger brother express himself in such a way brought tears of joy to my eyes, and I praised God for it.

On this particular day, William was giving a presentation in one of his classes when he suddenly collapsed. His heart had stopped beating – cardiac arrest. An eyewitness reported, "Junior was unconscious, and 9-1-1 was called." A nearby employee from the college heard the commotion and came quickly to the classroom to see if he could help. He successfully administered cardiac pulmonary resuscitation (CPR). The fire department and paramedics arrived on the scene quickly. They took Junior to a Birmingham, Alabama hospital by ambulance for evaluation and treatment.

The physicians could not explain what had caused his cardiac arrest. They ordered a cardiac catheterization to evaluate his heart anatomy.

From my family's point of view, this was just routine testing. My family didn't know it, but this was going to be a major event in their lives. At this point, even though I'm in the medical field, I also believed it was routine.

This hospital has a history with my family. It is the same hospital where William Sunday, Jr., was born on October 26, 1973. When Junior's heart stopped, my family was called. Immediately, they went to the hospital. My parents talked and joked with Junior. He requested a clean set of clothing because the CPR had disheveled his clothes. Although Junior didn't know it, he was very shortly going to need no earthly clothing. He would have heavenly attire and no more pain, fear or worries in this world. This reminds me that we do not know the day or hour when we take our last breath or the last time we will see or talk to our loved ones.

During the cardiac catheterization, the team discovered that Junior had an aortic dissection, which means blood was leaking from one of the major vessels in his body. The cardiologist and his team informed my parents that William needed to have emergency surgery to repair the dissection. My parents later recalled not really understanding what was happening. My sister, a family practice physician, knew this was a major surgery with serious potential complications. I acknowledged the procedure was serious as well. I said, "Lord, have mercy!"

As an anesthesiologist, this surgery was one of the most challenging emergency operations for administering anesthesia. There was a saying during my residency training that administering anesthesia for an aortic dissection or ruptured aortic aneurysm was "the granddaddy for precision and expertise." When presented with this type of procedure, normally, backup was called to have extra hands available to give assistance in the operating room. During the operation, the patient's blood pressure cannot be too high because it can extend the aneurysm and the patient will loose more blood – similar to a watering hose that has a hole in it. If you increase the flow of water, the amount of water will increase. In the same fashion, if the blood pressure is too low, vital organs like the brain, heart, kidneys and liver will have a decrease in their blood supply. This leads to dysfunction and organ failure.

While waiting for the next update, I went to God in prayer. I got on my knees in my hotel room and prayed for the healing of my brother, Junior, on this side of Heaven or in Heaven. Selfishly, I wanted it on this side of Heaven. I spoke of God's Will to be done in my brother's life. Whatever God wants – so be it. I began to cry, thinking of how young Junior was and how caring he was to his family and to everyone he met. I knew God had the last say in the matter.

I opened my Bible to speak the Word and pray for my family in this trying time. The entire chapter of Psalms 91 came to mind. This scripture refers to knowing that when I dwell in the secret place of the Most High God, I abide under His shadow. God is my refuge and fortress. God is my God, and I trust Him. God is everything I need. God always sends a person in my life to help and assist with life's issues and demands. When trials and tribulations come into my path, He shall deliver, cover, and protect me with His feathers because, under His wings, I'll trust. When I call Him, He will answer and deliver me from it all.

My faith in God assured me that God knows what's best. I also believed that whatever trial or situation came to my family's path, God had already equipped us to handle the situation. I continued to read the Word of God. *God is always present and my Source of strength and peace. I knew my God would keep me in perfect peace when my mind was focused on Him and the things of God* (Isaiah, 26:3). He will always help me, and I will not fear. I cast my burdens on Him, and I was confident that He would sustain me (Psalm 55:22). I'm truly grateful that I am never out of His presence (Psalm 139:7-10). I prayed without ceasing.

I called a friend, "Steph," short for Stephanis, to pray and keep me focused.

"Hello, Steph, how are you? My brother is in the hospital. He is in surgery now for a dissecting aorta," I said.

"Oh, my God! Hang in there. God is always in control," Steph said with confidence.

I began to cry, and Steph proceeded to pray. "God, You know what's going on with Junior at this time. God, You are our Healer and Deliverer. Strengthen the family at this time and strengthen Renee right now in the Name of Jesus. Renee, always remember, when circumstances seem overwhelming, don't look at what's going on around you; look at God. He is the author and finisher of our faith." I was extremely grateful for her help.

I said, "I know God has the last say in this situation. God knows what is best." With peace in my heart and mind, I told Steph, "All is well."

Steph replied, "Yes. Amen."

As soon as I finished the call with Steph, another friend, Benjil, called. She, too, sensed from my tone of voice that I was troubled.

Benjil said, "All is well." I told her what was happening in my life. With a confident voice, Benjil said to me, "God is always in control. It doesn't matter what it looks like. God will always be in control."

I replied, "I have confidence in Him that if I ask anything according to His Will, I know He hears me." Therefore, whatever I ask in Jesus' Name, I know God has already made a way. God sent Jesus to us so that we can go directly to Him in prayer, and He would hear me (1 John 5:14-15).

I thanked God again for allowing me to have friends to help and comfort me at this time. Friends whom I can call or go to, and be real with, are a treasure from God. They will not judge or put you down. They will speak kind words and encouragement. I truly thank God for two doves named Steph and Benjil for being there for me during this trying time.

I knew that prayer was a Christian's tool for talking to God, to acknowledge Him, and worship Him. God always answers prayer. Prayer is a communication with God in the Name of Jesus. Praying is talking with God, but doing more listening than talking. In addition, it is important to give thanks for what He has done through salvation, and to thank Him for His Son, Jesus. Praying kept my mind at peace, and blocked negative thoughts from entering my mind. God is faithful and just. He hears and answers all prayers. (I Thessalonians 5:17).

Life has many circumstances that will come my way. I stood firm on the Word of God. I stood still because I knew God was God all by Himself. *Be still and know that I am God* (Psalms 46:10). *He will never leave thee, nor forsake thee.* (Hebrews 13:6). Through prayer, I gained peace, strength and the courage to continue. I prayed, "Lord, this is a tough situation. Guide and direct me, in Jesus' Name. Amen." No matter what it looked like, God is always in control. I gave thanks to God for blessing my family and me.

I stayed positive as I waited for an update from my family. Instead of going back to Florida where I worked, I called the airline to change my reservation to Birmingham to be with my family. The customer service representative at the airline was extremely polite and understood the urgency of changing my reservation. Changing my flight from Washington, D.C. to Birmingham accrued no charge. I was coded as an open reservation, which meant I could set the return date at my convenience. God is so awesome. He will work everything out. I didn't want to text or call San because she was comforting my parents.

During my wait, I was not in distress, I was at peace. I thought about all the happy times during family dinners at my parent's home. My goal was to focus on Jesus only. My mind was filled with peace. Being stressed would not make the matter better, but worse, because I was focusing on the wrong things.

I gazed out my hotel room window. I saw people from various walks of life walking on the street below me in a hurried fashion. I pondered where they were going, and what their destinations were. It could be home, work, a restaurant. Some probably didn't know where they were bound. As I sat there watching all those strangers walk by, I was reminded that Junior was saved, and he believed Jesus died for his sins, rose again, and sits on the right hand of the Father.

The next update came after several hours of waiting – five long hours to be exact. My cell phone rang. It was San. "They repaired the dissecting aorta with a Dacron graft, but the cardiac team had problems with Junior coming off of the cardiopulmonary bypass machine (CPB)." According to San, they had been trying without success for two hours. The team said they would continue their attempts, but Junior's heart was severely damaged. They didn't know if he would make it. The cardiac surgeon said he would check the coronary arteries to see if any of the vessels needed to be bypassed to increase blood flow to the heart.

I could visualize the graft and CPB machine. I have administered anesthesia several times for heart surgeries. I went through the different diagnoses in my mind to determine the reasons the surgical team would use to get him off CPB:

1. Is his blood pressure too low or too high?
2. Is his heart pumping blood appropriately?
3. Does he need blood?

4. Could it be an inflammatory response or stroke from prolonged CPB circulation, which can have organ manifestations ranging from minimal dysfunction to total organ failure (meaning the organ wasn't working at all)?

I believed the team would do their best for Junior. I also knew that God had the last say in the matter.

While I waited for the next update, I fell asleep with a peaceful mind and soul. God was with Junior. At midnight, my phone rang. It was San. "Junior is in the intensive care unit in critical condition." According to what I was told, my family now filled the entire waiting area. We all thanked God that Junior had made it out of the operating room. There was going to be a long road ahead because the surgery was long and difficult. Being an anesthesiologist, I knew there could be some complications to a prolonged emergent cardiac surgery. I stood on the Word of God that He would heal Junior.

I arrived in Birmingham early the next morning and went to my parents' home. As always, my parents greeted me warmly. My mother cooked an awesome breakfast – fluffy buttermilk pancakes, scrambled eggs, crispy bacon, and buttered toast. We ate together. San said, "The nursing staff informed me that the family may come and visit at any time." I didn't say a word, but my anesthesiologist's mind reflected back to a time when I had heard this before, when the patient was not expected to recover from the surgery. I said to myself, "Whatever God decides is all right with me." My parents were strong in their faith in God as they have been throughout my life. This time was no exception.

We went to the hospital. When I arrived in the room, I immediately scanned the monitors to see what the blood pressure, heart rate, and the cardiac parameters showed on the screen. The displayed measurements looked stable. I went to the bedside and said, "I'm here, Junior." He squeezed my hand, and I turned away from my family as a tear came from my eyes. Junior looked as if he was sleeping. I thought back to the last time I saw him, exactly one week before. I would have never imagined him to be in the intensive care unit.

Throughout the day, the staff continued to update us on his condition. I questioned the nursing staff about why Junior was not receiving blood or a medication to increase his blood pressure. The staff quickly called the cardiac team. They agreed with my judgement and his blood pressure improved. Junior did not receive any sedation for two days because the physicians wanted him to wake up, as did we.

By day two, Junior still had not awakened. His wife, children, and the whole family stayed endless hours at the hospital. My family and I read the Bible to him and talked about the good days. I knew that two to three days were sufficient time for all of the anesthesia medications to be out of his system, and he should wake up.

Yet, another day went by, and Junior still didn't wake up. We, as a family unit, stayed in prayer and stood on the Word of God and noted that it was God's Plan, not ours. He knows what's best. I could feel that I was not in an anesthesiologist/professional mode anymore, but in a sister's. I did not want Junior to suffer because of my selfish desire for him to recover. I wanted him to have no pain, despair or worries of this world. God knows what's best, and I wanted the same for my brother. Life is a joy, but the greatest joy of all is being with Jesus, which is the ultimate goal in life.

After a brain scan, it was determined that Junior had experienced not one, but three strokes. One was in the brainstem, and his brain had herniated. From a medical standpoint, my sister and I understood what that meant.

The cardiac surgeon requested a meeting with the family. We gathered in a small room – small enough to be a bathroom. There were two ministers present – one was the family pastor, and one was my cousin. They stood while the family sat in five pastel upright, comfortable chairs. The reflection from the lamp in the room resembled a sunset on a peaceful evening on the beach. The ambiance of the room brought a sense of peace and love. The cardiac surgeon and nursing staff walked into the room. The surgeon kneeled on one knee and rested one of his arms on his knee. He said, "The life support needs to be removed because Junior won't wake up or recover. He has no brain activity." The surgeon continued, "Do not despair as the decision has already been made. William is already with God."

The room was so quiet I could hear my heart racing – similar to a car at the speedway. The precious memories of the many times I had been in the midst of surgeries on the heart flashed before my eyes. We, as people, take life for granted. It was an honor to provide anesthesia to my patients. My heavy eyelids closed, and I had a glimpse of Junior running through the glistening white gates of Heaven. I smiled; my little brother had completed his God-given Plan for his life.

Two by two, we went in to see Junior. My mother said, "All is well. He is in a better place." Everyone agreed with her. When Junior passed, I gripped his hand and kissed his cheek as the ventilator was turned off. Without the breathing machine and the intravenous medications, Junior was not living. I remembered back to the times I had rendered anesthesia for organ procurement (organ donation). After the designated organs were removed by the transplant surgeons and the surgery was completed, the same thing occurred – the person was not living anymore.

To pronounce a person not living – legally dead in the medical field – there are policies and procedures in accordance with medical standards. During my critical care anesthesia fellowship, I learned and carried out pronouncements, which were extremely difficult for me to do. I was in the room when the time of death was determined for Junior, my baby brother. This was anesthesia on the front line. As knowledgeable as I was about the actions of the critical care team, this was an out-of-the-box experience for me on a personal, not professional level.

My heart was at peace, but I realized my baby brother had passed on to be in Heaven. I didn't understand why Junior had to die, but God knows what's best. His ways are not mine. Junior always gave to others. Even with his passing on from this Earth, he continued to do so. He donated the corneas of his eyes so someone else could journey through life with the gift of sight.

April 5, 2011 was a difficult experience for my family. Junior, known as the "gentle giant," passed from this Earth. He died from a broken heart, an aortic dissection. To the end of his life, he displayed love, compassion, and generosity to everyone who came into his path. But one to two years before April 5, his compassion rose to another level. He made a point to always be the one who said, "I love you" after a conversation. The last text I received from Junior was, "I'm proud of you."

His meals always provided a sensational amore to my nose and pure bliss to my taste buds. However, his specialties were spaghetti, lasagna, and macaroni and cheese. Junior was a magnificent chef, and he could prepare any type of food. He was a master with his hands. He could do anything from repairing a leaking pipe in the kitchen to automobile maintenance. He would go out of his way to help others in need.

He was laid to rest April 13, 2011, with a Celebration of Life service at my home church in Birmingham, Alabama. The services followed the traditional Baptist format, with the family processional, readings from the Scriptures of the Old and New Testaments, and then prayer. We sang my brother's favorite song, "Something About the Name Jesus."

Friends and associates shared their reflections of his kindness, compassion, love, and generosity toward others. Junior's boss, Mr. Campbell, stood to speak. He said, "Junior was always caring for others. He would tell the students to set goals in life and strive to obtain them. Junior was very compassionate to all his students and coworkers. Junior would say Mr. Campbell needed to rest and not work so much. Enjoy life. Junior constantly spoke of his family – wife, children, mother, father and sisters. It seems like his family was my family. The positive energy radiated from him, from his last name, Sunday, to his behavior."

Mr. Campbell began to cry. "Junior, I'll miss you. Love you, and God will comfort your family. Thank you," he said and returned to his seat. The kind words from Mr. Campbell about Junior brought comfort to the family. I glanced down the row. One by one, each family member smiled. It was a joy to have shared Junior with all of his friends and associates.

Then the Word of God was brought through prayer. The scripture text was from John 14:1, 6 – *Do not let your heart be troubled. You believe in and adhere to and trust in and rely on God; believe in adhere to and trust in and rely also on Me… Jesus said to him. I am the Way and the Truth and the Life; no one comes to the Father except by Me.*

The important points brought forth were:

1. Trust and rely on God.
2. Comfort and peace comes from God.
3. The only way to the Father comes through Jesus.

4. Jesus - the Way, Truth, and Life.

The Word of God will always comfort, encourage, remind, and even convict us to fall in line with God's Plan. Throughout the services, my family displayed a peacefulness. We were comforted because we knew Junior was enjoying Heaven. We all dressed in blue and black, which were his favorite colors. The casket was blue, and the surrounding flowers were blue with white accents. This service celebrated Junior's life. After the memorial service, the interment followed. His body was returned to the ground. Ecclesiastes 12:7 Cross Reference Scriptures- Ecclesiastes 3:20, Genesis 3:19, Job 34:15. Psalms 103:14.

The heart of the Celebration Service paid tribute to Junior's life and gave support to my family. Afterwards, we celebrated with a Repast, as it is coined by some, or just a dinner with loved ones and friends to commence this joyous occasion. One more soldier of Christ passed from this life into Heaven to peace. He no longer had to experience life's concerns or situations.

My family's church hosted the dinner. When we arrived in the dining area, our loved ones, church members, friends, and associates greeted us with hugs and kisses. The whole room smelled just like my mother's kitchen on Sunday after church. The smell of the food made my mouth water and brought me a peace of mind. The menu consist of Junior's favorite food – crispy fried and baked chicken, macaroni and cheese, collard greens, green beans, potato salad and buttered rolls. Delicious food was all around us. The dessert display brought out the kid in everyone. There were homemade pound cakes, pecan pies, sour cream pound cakes, red velvet cakes and many more. The families of the church had prepared the food.

During the dinner, two of my good friends, Celeste and Erica sat at the table with me. Erica had come up from Pensacola, Florida to support my family and me. Celeste resides in Atlanta, Georgia and had come over for the funeral. They displayed genuine generosity from the point when I first called about Junior's passing. Afterwards, they called or texted me every day to encourage me.

Both Erica and Celeste embraced me and said, "I love you; if you need anything let me know."

I replied, "Love you, too. Thank you both for driving so far to be here."

"Even though we don't talk every day, you are always in my thoughts and heart," Erica replied.

Celeste said, "That's right. Renee, you are our sister."

I replied, "Thank you so much. God bless you and your family."

The dinner, hugs, kisses, and the conversation brought comfort to my family and me. Laughter embraced with love and compassion showed by family, friends, and associates empowered us to continue our journey in life.

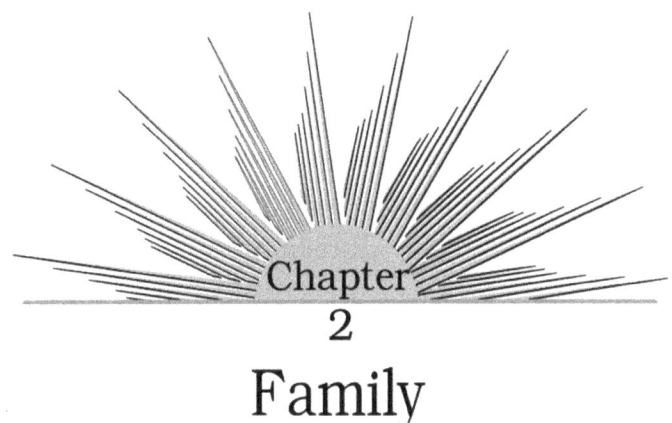

Chapter 2

Family

My parents, Mr. William Sunday, Sr., and Mrs. Rosetta Sunday, were born and raised in Alabama. They were reared in homes with Christianity as the backbone of their lives. Great wisdom, honesty, and truth were instilled in them at an early age. Prayer was established as an essential part of their lives and was passed on to us as their children. My parents always said, "Be thankful, be polite, be honest, and be steadfast, and immovable in goals and dreams of life. Always remember to help others in need."

As long as I can remember, my sister, San, has been my role model. She has always shown me love and set a good example to follow. Now as a wife and mother of two wonderful children, she continues to reveal what was instilled in her as a child. Her home is a home of prayer and love. My family has and always will continue to demonstrate our strong Christian foundation. But Junior's passing was truly a difficult time for all of us.

What is death and grief? A cliché we so often use is, "They are in a better place." My family and I are Christians and believe this statement. We know God's Plan is best, and Heaven is a real place with no pain, despair or grief. There is peace and rest from the journey here on Earth. The glorious, majestic, enthralling, and magnificent splendor of God in Heaven flows for eternity. Man embraced the unconditional love of God by accepting His love, joy, and peace on Earth. Earth is only a reflection of Heaven. My spiritual soul knows Junior is at peace and enjoying Heaven. Everyone reacts or responds to death and grieves differently.

Grief is a normal response to the death of a loved one, close associate, or friend. When coping with a death, there are emotional, physical, and spiritual responses. This can leave you feeling sad, angry, cheated, relieved, guilty, empty, shocked, and confused. I experienced a mixture of all of these emotions. I am a strong tower in my family, and at the same time, I was experiencing emotions I had never felt or dreamed of before.

I experienced several emotions and physical symptoms at one time. When I saw my brother's body in the casket arranged for the family's viewing , my mind, soul, and body collided together. I remembered back to what my mother had said, "I wished it was me instead of my baby." I felt the same way. The next thing I knew, I was sitting in a chair with a cool wet cloth on my forehead.

My mother said, "Renee, drink some water."

I replied, "What's wrong?"

My mother, sister, and the funeral home director said at the same time, "You fainted."

I gazed to my right, and my father was sitting in a chair. His eyes filled with tears. My family embraced each other. The room was quiet with low lighting and soft music playing in the cadence of, "Yes, Jesus Loves Me." A peaceful presence radiated among my family. One of the lights in the room aligned just right to gleam onto Junior's face; what a big smile he had.

My mother and father together said, "Everything will be all right."

The rest of the family replied, "Yes."

The funeral home director asked if we were happy with the appearance of Junior's body.

We were extremely pleased. Junior's face displayed peace, and the peace of God was with my family and me.

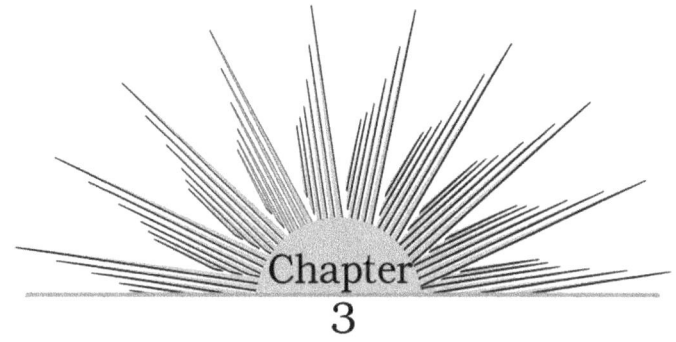

Chapter 3
Emotional Response

Let's examine the word "emotion." Emotions are complex experiences within an individual's state of mind interacting with internal and external influences. Everyone has emotions. They can be positive or negative. The goal is to turn a negative into a positive emotional state. The mind will do whatever it is programmed to do. If one says, "I am nothing," over and over in his or her mind, then eventually, that person will say something negative in response to that internal voice. The individual will be acting out of the belief system that was rehearsed and created.

According to the Word of God, the entire book of Galatians 5 relates to emotions. (Galatians 5:16-25). Apostle Paul explains that a believer will display fruit of the Holy Spirit, which include love, joy, patience, peace, kindness, goodness, faithfulness, and self-control. When I live and walk by the Holy Spirit, my guidance is from the Holy Spirit, and I am in tune to God's Plan for my life. I read the Word of God to gain understanding, and then the Holy Spirit will give me direction and lead me to make the right decisions.

The Holy Spirit is the comforter that God gave all. A part of Him is with us all of the time. Like unto an eagle, the Holy Spirit is an Eagle representing spiritual protection, bringing strength, courage, wisdom, healing, creation, and knowledge of all things.

The Eagle has:

1. An ability to see hidden spiritual truths, rising above the material to see the spiritual.
2. An ability to see the overall plan. The Spirit guides and teaches me.
3. Great power, balance, and dignity with grace.

The Holy Spirit will always reveal the pertinent information that is needed for every given situation. When I'm in doubt, I ask the Holy Spirit, and it shall be given unto me. The Holy Spirit, through the Word of God, will remove scales from my eyes. Then the truth of life can be revealed in my life. I can understand *who* I am, and *whose* I am. I'm learning that God's Plan is always the best plan. I trust Him and I do not lean to my own understanding; surely all things will fall in line.

Day by day as I travel through life, mountains high and valleys low, I know whatever comes my way:

1. It is common to all people.
2. God is faithful.
3. God has already provided a way of escape.
4. Every situation that comes my way, I can handle or bear.

Wow, sometimes it is hard to believe I can handle it. I'm so glad God is the potter, and I'm the clay. He is the Master of everything. I trust God. He provided a way before, and He will do it again. My development of trust in God goes from one level to the next. When I study the Bible, hear the Word, and apply the Word to my life, my relationship with God strengthens. My confidence in Him grows like a palm tree. The seed is planted, then the root system develops. Nourishment for the tree comes from water. It becomes tall and strong as the years go by. (1 Corinthians 10:13). I can't live without Him. He is my joy and peace. I'm nothing without God.

I had to renew my mind during this painful time. I was reminded of God's Plan, not my plan. I can truly say my emotions tried to get me down during my brother's death. God gave comfort to my family and me by reminding us that this is a transitional place called Earth. Everyone will experience death. I focused instead on celebrating Junior's life, and controlling my emotions with the Word of God. Speaking positive words goes a long way. While growing up, my parents always said that I was smart, beautiful, more than a conqueror, and I could do all things through Christ who strengthens me. I began to believe what my parents instilled in me, and a positive mindset became my motto in life.

The Word of God shows me what God says I am in Him. There are several steps to achieving peace through God's Word. To begin, I must: 1) receive what the Bible says, and 2) take a step further by believing what is said, and then 3) say and do what I believe. Which will allow God to shine through me, as the world views this positive glow I will be able to give others insight and encouragement. This will be a divine and awesome opportunity to spread the Good News about God and how He always makes a way.

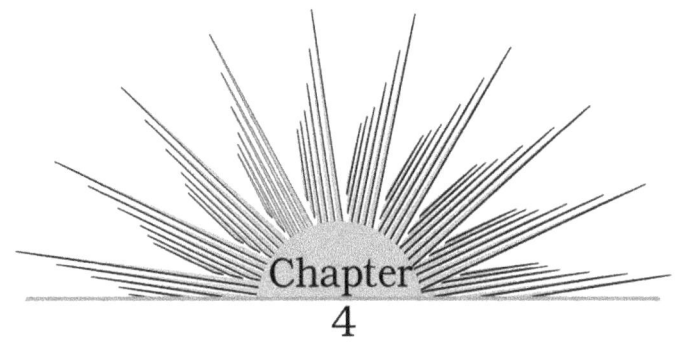

Chapter 4
Physical Response

During the grieving process, there can be a physical reaction. This reaction can lead to problems such as insomnia (not sleeping), pain, nausea, early satiety (eating less and feeling full quickly), or excessive eating or drinking. After my brother's death, I experienced headaches, nausea, and overeating, mostly junk. Our strong family bond kept me from going crazy, and losing my mind. The grieving process takes time and healing. It is a step-by-step process. Our physical body is a wonderful creation. The body responds to what our brain (mind) is thinking. If we are happy, our body is happy. If we are sad or hurting, our body is, too. As a part of my medical training, I had to take many classes. Three are relevant to speak of right now: anatomy, neuroanatomy and physiology. When it comes to emotions, whether they are positive or negative, the body will respond.

*****

Does the Body Respond to Emotions?

Let's use sadness as an example, resulting from a death in the family, or the death of a friend or an associate. There will be a response in the physical body. This can be seen when the body is in a state of fight or flight, which is a reaction to a highly emotional or stressful situation. The initial fight or flight signal comes from the brain, which activates the body to release the hormone, adrenaline, into the blood.

This hormone called 'adrenaline' will cause a cascade of events in the body. The pupils of the eyes dilate. Hair stands on end. The chest expands to increase the volume of air and oxygen in the lungs. The heart increases the volume of blood going in and out of the heart. The heart pumps faster, and blood pressure goes up. The muscles of the body and the blood vessels of the skin contract. The skin will look pale. The liver will release glucose, which provides fuel for the muscles. Please do not tell my professors that I simplified the body's response to stress into one paragraph. It is not that simple. The human body is complex, and what we think in our mind affects our physical being.

The human body responds to our emotions in many ways. The quicker we control our emotions in an effective manner, the quicker our bodies will line up to our minds. During my family's grieving process, our strong Christian foundation kept us stable and relative healthy. The process takes time, and it is a step-by-step process. Everyone involved will respond differently in regard to his or her emotional and physical responses. The human body responds to what we see, hear, smell, and touch.

As I have learned during the grieving process, a few steps are important:

1. Visit with family, friends, and associates to comfort each other. A smile and a hug bring joy. Showing love is the best way to show support.

2. Extend a helping hand to the family, no matter how big or small. It will be appreciated and treasured.

3. Hearing (Listening) – The family needs to hear expressions of kind words about how God will comfort and keep them. Celebrate the life of the person who died. To hear that the person is in a better place with no more cares of the world brings peace to the heart.

4. Smell and Taste – The smell of flowers brings a sense of peace, joy, and relaxation to the person that's remaining on Earth to live and achieve their goals and dreams. With my traditional Christian background, I appreciated people visiting and bringing tokens of love – mostly food, plants, and sympathy cards. This was a gracious gesture because I chose to eat the wrong foods in the beginning of my grieving process, and my family made sure I made better selections. As we breathe in and out, the sense of smell reminds us of the beauty of this world.

5. Touch – A hug goes a long way. We saw how my brother touched so many lives. He

showed love to everyone. It brought joy and peace to my family and me. Extending an expression of love, such as a hug and a handshake, shows compassion for others.

All of our senses feed into our mind and the cascade process begins. Speak and think positively. This will trigger positive responses in our human body. God is always Good. He will comfort and heal us throughout the grieving process.

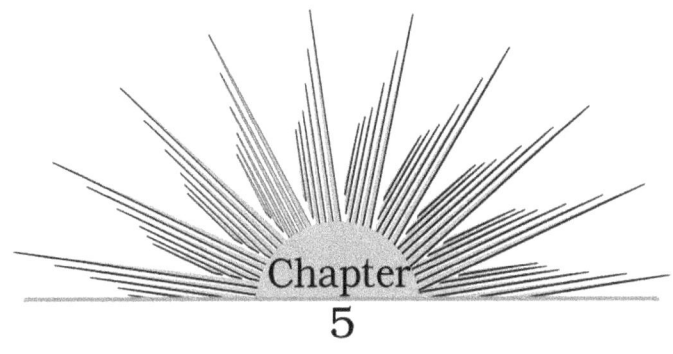

Chapter 5
Spiritual Response

The spiritual response to death can range from questioning your beliefs, and feeling disappointed about your religion, to feeling stronger about your beliefs and faith.

Now, I, of course, felt something different. I thought I had let God and my brother down. Maybe I did not pray the right prayer or did not intercede the right way, or I had not asked God with faith of healing. I actually felt fragmented because I was experiencing so many different emotions at one time.

Fortunately, as time went on my emotions and physical body proceeded through the grieving process. Every day was better and better. One day the nausea was there, and the next day it was gone. I experienced peace, and it continued. Then the peace of God was evident in my life. My family and I continued to say that Junior finally had peace. God did answer my prayers. His will came to pass. Junior's healing was done in Heaven.

My spiritual being was strong in the knowledge that God always knows what is best. There are many events and occurrences in my life I don't understand. But I trust, rely, and depend on God because everything will work out for His honor and glory. My friends and associates said kind words and prayed for my family and me.

So what happened next? What were the steps my family and I took to move forward?

I did take some time off from work to reflect on our family's affairs. This was extremely important, because I had several emotions occurring at one time. My body was going through changes that I had not experienced before. My spirit knew Junior was in Heaven and would not have to experience the ups and downs of this world. But my heart hurt because Junior was my baby brother, and I loved and missed him so much. There were nights I cried myself to sleep, and other nights the tender voice of the Holy Spirit rocked me to sleep.

Junior and I used to talk and text all the time. We would encourage each other to achieve and enjoy life to its fullest. I missed his loving contact.

Where did I turn? I went back to the basics. I went to the Word of God. I believed in God and that He had raised Jesus from the dead. I knew I was saved and God knows what is best. I searched the Word of God to bring back to remembrance God's Promises. God's Promises are vast – I just cannot recall them all, but they are found throughout the Bible.

At this point, I developed a journal with scriptures and made index cards. I repeated the scriptures and meditated on them. Reciting and speaking the Word of God fed me. Spending time with the Word of God reminded me that God gave His Only begotten Son so that I can have everlasting life. (John 3:16). God is my rock and salvation. (Psalms 89:26). When I need help, He is always with me. (Psalms 46:1).

Specifically, I went to the Bible, King James Version. I wrote down where the scripture was located, and then jotted down a sentence, about what God said I am in this particular passage. This is the result:

Genesis 45:18	Enjoy the best of the land
Deuteronomy 28:13	Head and not the tail
Romans 1:1	Set apart for God
Romans 4:20-22	Strong in Faith, Glory be to God ONLY
Romans 8:1	Free from Condemnation
Romans 8:16	Child of God
John 15:15	Friend of God
Matthew 5:13-14	Salt of the Earth
Romans 8:17	Joint heir with Christ
Romans 8:37	Overcomer
2 Corinthians 5:21	Righteous of God
1 Corinthians 3:17	Temple of God
1 Corinthians 3:9	Coworker with God
1 Corinthians 6:20	Bought with a Price
2 Corinthians 1:21-22	Anointed, Sealed, Consecrated me
2 Corinthians 5:17-18	Reconciliation
Philippians 3:20	Citizen of Heaven

Philippians 4:13	Christ which strengthens me
Ephesians 2:6	Sitting with Christ in Heaven
Ephesians 2:10	Workmanship
Ephesians 2:18	Access through the Blood
Colossians 1:14	Redeemed and Forgiven

These are a few of the scriptures that tell me who I am in Christ. My daily commitment was to read and meditate on the Word, to speak confessions of Faith, praying and communing with God in the Name of Jesus and hearing the Word of God.

Through my diligence in the Word of God, the Holy Spirit comforts and guides me. When a situation or trial comes, draw nearer (closer) to God because He has already made a way out of it. There has to be a test before a testimony develops. God reveals Himself in every situation. Reference Scripture: All things work together for good to them that love God, to them who are called according to His Purpose (Romans 8:28).

Now let's get back to the comfort cards. I made some flash cards with scriptures on the index cards so I could review the Word at any given moment. I call them *Sunday Comfort Cards*. I put the scripture on one side and the chapter and verse identification on the other side. I used some of the above scriptures and added more as time progressed.

To list a few:

- ❖ For I know the plans I have for you declares the Lord, plans to prosper you and not to harm you, plans to give you an expected end. (Jeremiah 29:11)
- ❖ Call unto me, and I will answer, thee and show thee great and mighty things, which thou knowest not. (Jeremiah 33:3)
- ❖ Beloved, I wish above all things that thou mayest prosper and be in good health, Even as thy soul prospereth. (3 John 2)
- ❖ Be not deceived; God is not mocked: for whatsoever a man soweth, that shall He also reap. For he that soweth to his flesh shall of the flesh reap corruption; But he that soweth to the Spirit shall of the Spirit reap life everlasting. And Let us not be weary in well doing: for in due season we shall reap, if we faint not. (Galatians 6:7-9)

❖ Therefore take no thought, saying what shall we eat? or, what we drink? or, Wherewithal shall we be clothed? For after all these things do the heavenly Father knoweth that ye have need of all these things. But seek ye first the Kingdom of God, and His righteousness, and all these things shall be added unto you. (Matthew 6:31, 33)

❖ But my God will supply all of your needs according to His riches in glory by Christ Jesus. Now unto God and our Father be glory for ever and ever. Amen. (Philippians 4:19-20)

Meditating on the scriptures throughout the day and night gave me a sense of comfort and peace during my grieving process. My comfort cards could be quickly reviewed and recited during lunch, at the gym, and at any given time. The Word of God was present before me and helped me stay focused on Jesus. I missed Junior, but I knew he was in Heaven.

Hearing and reading the Word of God was an important part of my recovery process. The Word brought forth by the men and women of God enriched my soul, and renewed my mind. I continued to attend Bible study, mid-week service, Sunday service, and I viewed streaming online programs. The Word of God strengthened me during my grieving process. It was, and still is, my compass through life, and the light I follow throughout my journey.(Psalms 119:105) My peace and true freedom from the cares, injustice, and destruction of this world relies on hearing the Word and applying it to my life on a daily basis. I cast all of my burdens on Jesus because He cares for me. (1 Peter 5:7)

The Sunday Family has and will continue to have a strong Christian foundation. Junior's passing was a trying experience for us. Each of us displayed emotional, physical, and spiritual responses. The grieving process is different for every given person. It is okay to have different responses because everyone can and will react or channel stress in several ways. As a unit, the family stayed together and lifted each other up. We went to our foundation which is God's Word. God gave us comfort throughout the whole process, and today He is still giving us strength to continue on.

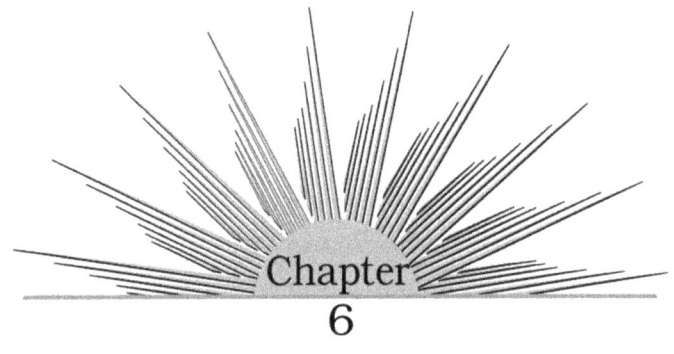

Chapter 6
Transition

To move on from any difficult time, there has to be an event of "transition." Transition is a term I coined for the event that must take place to pass beyond the trying experience. A transition event occurs after I have experienced the emotional, physical, and spiritual responses to grief. Then I realized and gained a revelation that Junior would want me to enjoy life and accomplish my goals and dreams. A transition can be going back to work, developing a new hobby, or moving into a new home. The most helpful part of a transition event is to be pampered, to gain a sense of newness and peace about life, and to truly engage in balanced and enjoyable activities.

Pamper yourself with a sense of appreciating your wellness of body and mind. The goal of transitioning is to feed the mind with positive influences. As for the Sunday family, my parent's transition event was moving into their new home. Before my brother passed, this was already in the works. The sense of the newness of the environment gave peace and a wellness to their mind. Junior saw the home the day before he transitioned from this Earth.

The process of transitioning has no time frame, and can be different for everyone.

For San and I, the transition events were similar; we went back to work in the medical field. The compassion and dedication of serving and being a part of the healing process of others brings joy, peace, and wellness of mind.

During my first week back at work, I had a patient named Beverly Smith (not her real name), whose son passed, years ago after a terrible car accident. Beverly was there to have a colonoscopy to evaluate her symptoms of constipation and abdominal pain. Beverly spoke of his kindness and laughter, and how her son always made others laugh. I shared with Beverly my experience and journey with the Lord during my grieving process. She smiled and said, "I will do the same. I will make some comfort cards, and make a plan of action toward transitioning." We prayed together. After the prayer, Ms. Smith said, "I'm ready to eat and go home."

I said, "Ms. Smith, you haven't had your procedure."

Ms. Smith said, "I'm already healed."

I said, "Yes. Amen." I proceeded to ask are you ok?

Ms. Smith replied, "Yes, great. Thank you, Dr. Sunday"

I smiled. "You're welcome." Ms. Smith held my hand as she went to sleep for the procedure.

The results of the colonoscopy were normal. No explanation or evidence to answer the question of constipation and abdominal pain. Ms. Smith was right. She was already healed. I was overjoyed to be a part of the plan to help someone else using my experiences.

One of my mother's greatest pearls of wisdom is when you go through situations or troubles, it is to help someone else with the same or similar situations. I was truly grateful that God trusted me to help one of His precious people here on Earth.

As I walked through the halls of the operating room and provided anesthesia, I did not falter or have doubts. God inspired me to continue on and to move forward. It took time for my diet to return to high protein and low carbohydrate. Yet, I craved Chinese food. Once a week, I yearned for sweet and sour chicken with the dazzling succulent red sauce, and amazing shrimp fried rice. The owners of the restaurant, Mei and Wei were so pleasant. They recognized me every time I came in.

One Thursday morning, I awakened thinking about sweet and sour chicken and of course the red sauce. After work, my first destination was the Chinese restaurant. No question or debate ever entered my mind in carrying out this task. I entered the restaurant where I have eaten many times before. The owners recognized me.

"Hello, how are you?"

Before I could respond the telephone rang. Mei answered the phone. Suddenly, she was screaming and in tears. She dropped the telephone and ran outside. I followed her out and found her sitting on the sidewalk.

"Mei, what's wrong?" I asked.

Mei answered, "My father just died from stomach cancer."

I hugged Mei as she cried.

I said, "It will be okay. It's okay to cry, Mei. I've been there."

Mei stopped crying. "What happens now?" she asked.

"That's a good question," I replied. Then I asked, "Do you believe in God, Mei?"

"Yes, I believe in God."

I replied, "Let's pray. Our Father, we come to you as humble as we know how, thanking You for being God and God all by yourself. Thank you for Your Grace and Love for us. I lift up Mei and her family to You for comfort, direction, and give them peace in this trying time. Lord, we do not understand so many things in our lives. Thank you for knowing what's best for us. God's Plan is not our plan. Strengthen Mei and her family to stand on the Word during the passing on of their loved one. Thank you, Lord Jesus, who died for our sins. We touch and agree in Jesus' Name, Amen. Amen. Amen."

Mei said, "Thank you so much. I will make it through. I love my father and I will miss him."

I said, "Yes, you will. Mei, celebrate your father's life. Reading the Word of God and prayering will give you peace to continue to move forward. Call me if you need me. I can come by to talk or just say nothing. We can just sit and listen to the birds sing. Love you, Mei."

Mei, replied, "Love you."

I returned to my car.

Mei called out to me. "Renee, you forgot your food."

I replied, "Lord have mercy." I had forgotten all about the sweet and sour chicken. We both laughed.

"Good bye, Renee. See you next week."

I said, "Okay. Everything will work out, Mei."

I sat in my car amazed at how I had planned to enjoy a meal, but God had a bigger, more important plan. He used me to assist Mei in her time of need.

Lord, thank You for using me in Your Plan. My experience with grieving for Junior enabled me to stand and intercede for someone else. As I glanced into the sky, there was the most beautiful rainbow I have ever seen. A sense of peace was all around me and my eyes filled with tears.

My transition events became vast. Now what does that mean?

I learned how to pamper myself.

Pampering helps us gain a better appreciation of the body and surroundings. Being pampered begins at the top of the head and extends to the soles of the feet. The following are examples of what I chose in my quest to appreciate my body and surroundings.

Dawn of the morning, so bright with a celestial fragrance of fresh dew drops seemed to bring reincarnation to life. The joy of the day brings a new opportunity to enjoy life's pleasures.

Aromatherapy is the use of essential oils from plants, spices, and flowers. The oils produce a fragrance that can provide a sense of well-being and an experience of relaxation and wellness. A sense of well-being and calmness encamped me when I smelled the fragrance of lavender, which is my favorite essential oil. The use of aromatherapy enhanced the realization of how the human body and mind are so intertwined together. The physical, emotional, and spiritual well-being are all at work at the same time. When I inhale the aroma of essential oils, the emotional center of my brain is affected. The sense of smell is the only one of the five senses directly related to the limbic lobe of the brain which is the emotional control center. All of the other senses: touch, taste, hearing and sight, are directed through another part of the brain- the thalamus, then passing a stimulus to cerebral cortex and other parts of the brain.

The redolence of the essential oils brought a state of peace to my mind. To enjoy a warm bubble bath with lavender candles reduced my stress. It aided me in sleeping, boosted my joy and divine awareness and perception of God's protection. It empowered me with a sound mind, body, and soul.

I went a step further to maximize the benefits of essential oils. I scheduled biweekly massage therapy sessions. My massage therapist was, and still is, one of my angels from God. The tranquil music of serene waves flowing on the beach, carefree white birds flying in the sky, and the radiant glow of the sun on the water created a perfect match to set the ambiance of peace, joy, and love. This magnificent picture transcended my mind and brought remembrance of God's unconditional love. He loves me. The session involved a one-hour massage with application of superficial and deep rhythmic compression.

Through transformation, my cat scratched cheeks began to diminish, solid rock neck began to relax and turtle-shelled back finally returned to reveal my suave muscles. The massage reestablished humility, awareness, peace and joy in my mind and body. I was rejuvenated into a gentle lamb.

God's love and compassion was the ultimate divine sacrifice of His Son Jesus as the Lamb of God. (John 1:29). Jesus came and paid for the sins of the world with His life. Then Jesus arose in three days and ascended to the right hand of God in Heaven. He sent His Holy Spirit to believers like me to empower us to live and to teach the message of salvation. The peace and goodness of God renewed my mind, body, and soul. I had and still have confidence that God will always be my guiding star.

Another transition example was accomplished as I gained a better sense of appreciation of how beautiful and wonderful the world is. To look and see how God has it all together is a WOW moment. Every living thing has a place, position and purpose in life. From the smallest animal to the existence of mankind, we interact and rely on each other. To look and see how the birds fly and how the clouds move throughout the land is wonderful. I look at life a little different after going through the grieving process. I have stopped focusing on my plan and shifted to God's Plan for my life and surroundings. I changed my prayer focus, because really I was begging God to change my situations. God is the Lord of my life's journey and I am a steward of His plan and timing. After my "light bulb" event, I realized that I have to go through trials and situations to learn, mature, and develop in my walk with God and to trust, depend, and rely on Him.

My family and I had to go through this test – losing my brother – in order to have a testimony. We can truly say that God will always provide what's needed to set us free from the cares of the Earth. I regained my love for empowering others and this led to the igniting of my gift of writing. Just like a budding flower, my writing started as a method for expressing my grieving experience with my peers, and then emerged on paper for others to view. I can empower and help others going through the same or similar situations.

Life has many ups and downs, mountains and valleys. The way one conquers a task is to seek God first and the Holy Spirit will guide and direct every phase of the situation. God has already made a way out of every trial that comes our way.

(1 Corinthians 10:13 -*Amplified Bible): *For no temptation (no trial regarded as enticing to sin), [no matter how it comes or where it leads] has overtaken you and laid hold on you that is not common to man [that is, no temptation or trial has come to you that is beyond human resistance and that is not adjusted and adapted and belonging to human experience, and such as man can bear]. But God is faithful [to His Word and to His compassionate nature], and He [can be trusted] not to let you be tempted and tried and assayed beyond your ability and strength of resistance and power to endure, but with the temptation He will [always] also provide the way out (the means of escape to a landing place), that you may be capable and strong and powerful to bear up under it patiently. Trust and rely on God.*

Our lives are predestined and stated so eloquently in the Word, (Ephesians 2:10 *Amplified Bible): *For we are God's own handiwork – His workmanship, recreated in Christ Jesus – born anew – that we may do these good works which God [predestined (planned beforehand) for us (taking paths which He prepared ahead of time), that we should walk in them [living the good life which He prearranged and made ready for us to live].*

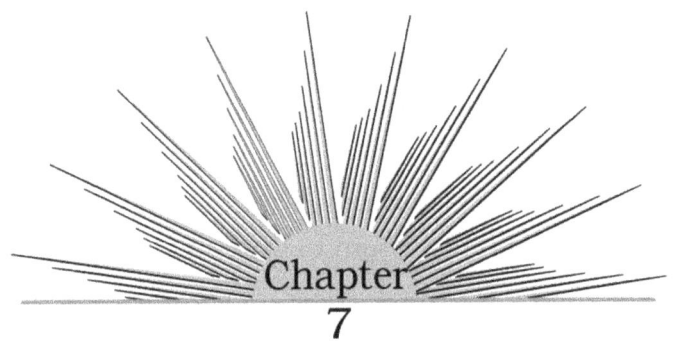

Chapter 7
Faith and Anesthesia

I walk softly along this pathway of peace and harmony to be used as an instrument of God's Plan - being a part of the healing process of the awesome creation of mankind.

The practice of anesthesia is a very rewarding field. I have been practicing anesthesia for over thirteen years. I was inspired to choose the path of anesthesia during my sophomore year of college. I had the honor of participating in a summer program to encourage minorities and women to pursue a career in the medical field. As a partner in my classes, I was paired with Joy, an anesthesiologist.

Joy was a married woman with children. She was very family-oriented. In 1988, she valued being one of the few females in anesthesia. Joy was part of the plan to bring unspeakable joy to my life. I treasured the time I spent with her. I was always very early – to be exact, one hour early – for our scheduled meeting time. I was so excited to be in the operating room to look and see all of the occurrences that took place before, during, and after surgery. All of the staff was extremely kind to me. I asked many questions. I thought I was being a pest, but I received a lot of encouragement from the staff. They encouraged me along the way to ask, ask away.

One nurse said, "You'll be an awesome anesthesiologist because you listen to the patients."

I have replayed this statement throughout my training and now, at times, I still hear it. My goal is to be part of God's Plan to provide the service of anesthesia. I bring comfort and peace to my patients. I had the privilege of seeing Joy again about two years ago at an anesthesia conference in the same city where we met.

I thanked Joy for being a part of God's Plan in my life. Now, I empower people everywhere I go. It brought tears to her eyes to know she had made such an impact in my life.

She smiled from ear to ear and said, "God bless."

My soul jumped for joy and I replied, "Same to you."

Throughout my journey, I was always encouraged by my family. My parents instilled in me at an early age that I could accomplish all things through Christ. My family prayed and inspired me along the way. San, my sister, was four years ahead of me in school. At the same time I was graduating from college, she was graduating from medical school. I was always peeking in her books and reading through her medical school books. I was the typical whiny little sister and always in the way. San loved me, so she put up with me. She didn't realize that I was learning in advance of my career in the medical field. She was molding my life one day at a time.

The art of providing anesthesia in my case was a thirteen year voyage, with four years of college, four years of medical school, and four years of residency and one year of a critical care fellowship. My skills began as a seed and grew to an amazing and beautiful flower.

The past thirteen years have gone by so fast, I still remember the days of medical school and residency. On many days, I had to be up 24 hours, and it seemed as though the day would never end. Those days became weeks and then months and years. Through it all, I have never forgotten the words that have been spoken to encourage me.

Anesthesia is a very serious and dynamic field of medicine. Providing anesthesia to patients is part of God's healing process. Patients are comfortable and not aware of the task that's taking place. Anesthesia is the state or condition of a loss of sensation – pain and reversible consciousness. The expertise of the team is at work through the Grace of God. Their hands are performing the Will of God.

The majority of surgical patients are nervous and anxious about having surgery or a procedure. The patients have to be "NPO," meaning nothing per orifice (nothing per mouth). They have to endure going without anything to drink or eat for two to eight hours before the procedure or surgery. It is difficult to give up food and drink, even if only temporarily. I know. I have experienced this myself, but it is extremely important. If this goal is not maintained, the risks associated with anesthesia increase for the patients.

Every morning before work, I pray for my patients and their families, I ask for healing of their bodies and pray that whatever is wrong God will make right. Everyone who comes into their path will be of God Only.

When I meet my patients, I greet them with a smile and introduce myself as Dr. Sunday, the anesthesiologist. Just to hear my name brings a sense of peace and occasionally laughter to my patients. Questions about the patient's height and weight or his or her ability to perform basic daily activities such as walking up and down stairs and preparing meals are obtained before surgery or a procedure. A physical examination is done from the top of the head to the soles of the feet. The majestic rhythm of the heart and royal lung sounds exemplifies how wonderful and magnificent the body is made.

Before induction or the start of anesthesia, the appropriate monitors are placed. I inform the patient it is time for nighty-night or go to sleep; the team will take very good care of them. A majority of the patients smile or say, "Thank you" or both. Patients sense a calm and peaceful environment.

Undergoing surgery or a procedure with anesthesia has risks. These substantial risks can range from nausea and vomiting to injury or damage to all of the vital organs – lung, liver, heart, kidneys, spinal cord and brain. The field of anesthesia specifically has improved dramatically with new technology such as ventilators and medications with fewer side effects and complications. The risk of anesthesia can depend on the type of surgery and the type of anesthesia administered. The patient's medical history and physical state, such as whether they are hydrated or dehydrated, are very critical information.

The timing of the surgery and anesthesia is also vitally important. Elective and emergent surgeries are like a sunrise and sunset – very different. Emergent means the surgery has to be done right away to save a patient's life or to decrease further insult of the injury to the body. In my days of working in the trauma world – meaning I was the anesthesia provider on call for patients needing emergency surgeries—sometimes there was only an opportunity to ask the patient if they had any allergies to medications. At times the only information was from the paramedics' team. The anesthesia providers are the gatekeepers of the operating room. The goal is to know what's going on in every organ and system of a patient's body.

When I administer anesthesia, it is like I'm taking care of a family member. My goal is to exceed the expectations of my patient and their family, and of course, to meet the standard of care. I am proud of my skill-set and confidence, and I feel rewarded when my patients are satisfied with their care.

Junior's surgery was an emergency: the surgery had to be done right away. His aorta was dissected. The aorta is the major vessel (artery) that transports blood and oxygen to all parts of the body, except specific areas of the lungs. The aorta begins in the heart, the left ventricle to be exact, and extends into the abdomen of the body, the area between your chest and pelvis – close to your belly button.

An aortic dissection occurs when there is a tear in the walls of the aorta, which causes blood to be forced through the hole and the hole becomes bigger. The result is similar to the blowout of a tire when it occurs. There's a sudden release of air, but in the case of an aorta it is blood. This is just a brief overview of an aortic dissection. My colleagues will forgive me for being so brief. It was truly a blessing for my parents to talk to Junior when he was in the emergency department before the surgery because this turned out to be their last time laughing with him.

God's Plan for our life is what's best for us. I administer anesthesia because God has given me the knowledge, wisdom, passion and zeal to do the job with a spirit of excellence. I do not take this opportunity for granted. I give God all of the praise and honor for it. Trusting, believing, and having faith in God, and being an anesthesiologist goes hand and hand in my life. God has blessed me and will continue to bless me with the spirit of excellence that flows in everything I do and say. He has blessed all the work of my hands. (Deuteronomy 28:12).

I rely and depend on God and I represent Him through my career of anesthesia. Some patients are terrified about surgery or having a procedure. It is an awesome find to have a caring and humble anesthesia provider in the midst. When patients awake, there is a sigh of relief in their eyes. One of my goals in life is to render the best anesthesia service to all patients who come into my path. Anesthesia and Faith are exceeding joyful and joyfully divine.

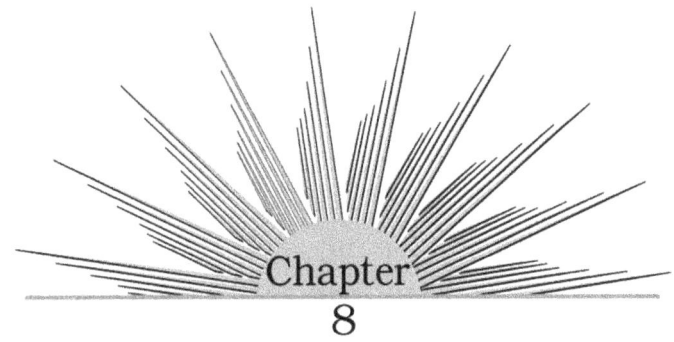

Chapter 8
A Mother and Father's Love

Junior was my parents' only son. In fact, my mother's physician didn't want my parents to have any more children, because my mother experienced gestational diabetes when I was born. But my parents deeply wanted a boy to be named after my father. They prayed about it and Junior was born with no problems with him or my mother. God blessed us with Junior.

As my mind goes back to a time when my mother was changing my brother's diaper, it is merely a glimpse of a memory from so long ago. I was only five, but I would help my mother by getting a diaper for Junior. I was a busybody, and my parents would always make me feel like I had done a great deed. After I got his diaper, I'd have a big smile on my face because I was his big sister who came to the rescue.

Memories blow by so quickly, like crisp leaves on a breezy fall day. One minute San, Junior, and I were playing in the front yard with our bicycles, and the next day we were graduating from high school. It feels like yesterday, all of us laughing at the kitchen table, because when we visited as adults our mother always put some money in our pockets or gave us food to take home. Years progressed and took off, especially when love was bountiful and shown by my parents.

My mother is a strong lady with the instinct about what to do in every situation or concern that arrives. She also has the wisdom about what not to do. A gentle, victorious pearl that God blessed our Sunday family with, and a gleaming light to follow; her life paints a classy gem of grace.

My father is our protection, strength, and the foundation of the Sunday family. Compassion and gratitude for our fellow man emerges from our walk with God and our father's life's journey.

When Junior passed, my mother was the first one to say, "All is well." But she told me later, "I wish it was me, not my baby." This whisper from my mother, I barely understood. She said, "He was just in my arms, then the patter of feet, and now with God and all of His Glory."

I grasped the meaning of my parents' being guardian angels from God to nurture and protect their children. This unconditional love between a mother and father and son is like a rainbow after a spring shower – a gift from God with expressions of His love, wisdom, and protection.

My parents said, "God knows best, and Junior is in a better place. He has no sorrow, no pain or despair in Heaven." God is giving them peace day by day. This was a very trying time for my parents. God comforted them and will continue to do so. We encouraged each other day in and day out. We leaned on each other while leaning on God. They trust Him and depend on Him. As I perceive the world through their eyes, this is what I see and what they are saying through their eyes:

~A Mother's Love~

A mother's love never ends.
A mother's love never bends.
When you took your first breath, I knew within,
That God had entrusted me to guide you until the end.
My love was with you in the good and the not so good times.
Your life was awesome to view because I knew you were a jewel within.

A mother's love never fades.
A mother's love never goes away.
I always prayed for you to obtain all your dreams.
The gleam in your eyes always brought a smile
To my heart, an everlasting glow.
You are enjoying Heaven with peace and joy

The heavenly courts to view and adore.
I miss you; I have peace to know you are in Heaven
You have obtained the ultimate goal of life,
To be with Our Heavenly Father, this is God Himself.

I cannot explain a mother's love,
But I know it goes beyond the skin of a man.
The heart of a mother never gives up
Because God is always in the Plan.

I do know God's Love lasts forever,
And forever I will remember your compassion for your fellow man.
My son, a mother's love is from God above to be your angel on Earth,
To love, cherish, and always to hold to the end.

Golden Pearl: God's Love never ends.
A Mother's Love never ends.

~A Father's Love~

A father's love so deep and true,
A father's love goes down to the bone.
We carry the same name with honor and dignity,
With one common goal to look upon Jesus' face.
You went before me not by my choice,
But I know God knows best in life.

My faith and trust in God and is my Rock in life.
You are in Heaven with its peace and joy.
You are free of pain and sad times too.
You are enjoying Heaven with a dance and praise.

We always talked about life.
I always said God will make a way.
The way was already prepared for you
To be a man with the name William Sunday.
You were a Junior to the world but for me
You were a legacy of strong men and a gentle spirit
That loved God with the last name Sunday.

A father's love stands firm forever and ever.
A father's love to you I promised God to do,
That I would be an example of a godly man.

I'm glad to say you were a man of love through and through.

My son, Enjoy Heaven with triumph and laughter.
You did your job with compassion and love.
To everyone who came in your path.
God is good and God is love.
A father's love is a gift from God.

Golden Pearl: God's Love never ends
A Father's Love never ends

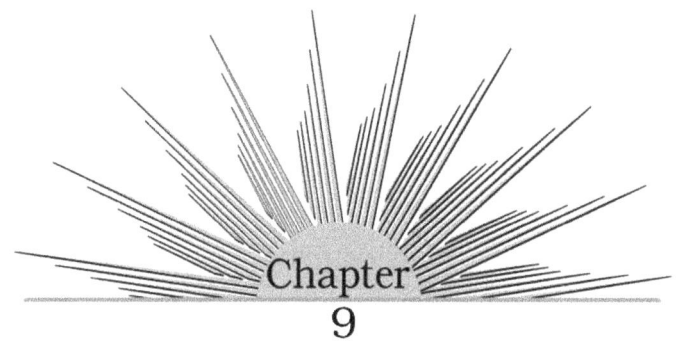

Chapter 9
Bringing It All Together

It's been over one year since my brother went to Heaven. Do I miss Junior? Do I get emotional at times? Yes, Yes. I know God's Plan is not my plan. God knows best and I have confidence in Him. There will always be situations I do not understand or cannot comprehend. God is comforting my family and me. We are enjoying life. We embrace each other and lean on God for direction and guidance every step of the way. Reading and meditating on the Word of God regulates and renews our minds. We trust God.

Trusting God does not mean the path is clear. He will align all of the necessary integrated pebbles one by one to form a unique path just for me. He is faithful to His Word. Life comes with dark clouds and problems, which is common to all people. God is my solid foundation. He gives me peace in Him. Even though I walked through the grieving process, I did not give up. My key to surviving this difficult experience was God. The ripples of water flowing from my eyes and rapid rhythms of my heart were rolled away by God. He reassured me along the peaceful shores. God was and will continue to be my only refuge through my troubled times.

Everyone copes with grief in diverse ways and responds differently. It is important to reach out to others like family, friends, the church, support groups, or professional therapists. Grief can last for weeks, months, and even longer depending on the relationship with the person who is deceased. Remember, grief is a normal process.

POINTS I LEARNED IN THE GRIEVING PROCESS THAT I WANT TO SHARE:

> ➢ Participate in memorial or funeral services, as this is a tribute to the person who died and you can be supportive for others.

> Be with family and loved ones. To be in company with family and loved ones will bring a sense of love, support, and well-being. Standing together and encouraging each other are true mottos to embrace every walk of life. The feeling of love will draw and set the atmosphere for peace, joy, and laughter.

> Allow yourself to have a transition event, where you pamper yourself, gain a sense of newness, and peace about life, and engage in balanced and enjoyable activities.

Listen, it is OK to cry. It is OK to ask why. It is OK express yourself. My family and I have a strong Christian foundation and it is OK to go through the grieving process. I saw how my family's faith in God and knowing without doubt or wavering that He does not make any mistakes comforted them. He is ALWAYS in control.

Life is worth living. I remember and celebrate Junior's life. I am smiling right now because I know he is enjoying Heaven. When I drive in traffic, or ride in an airplane, or relax in my home in my secret place, I know life is precious. I appreciate every day as if it was my last day on this Earth. Be it challenging or a difficult situation, or even a joyous situation, express love with everyone you come into contact with. Smile, and someone will smile at you.

Families are not alone in their grief. Doctors, nurses and medical support staff also grieve. Listen, healthcare providers – it is OK to cry, to ask why, and to express yourselves. We are part of the healing process of patients every day. We are in stressful careers. Life has ups and downs and valleys and mountains to conquer, but we have to relieve stress. My relationship with God makes the difference. My stress becomes rest through trusting, depending, and relying on God. He always gives me everything I need. I value my meditation every morning. It sets the tone for the day. The Holy Spirit guides and directs me throughout the day. I hear His voice when I need to be silent, talk, go or stay. My goal is to set the atmosphere of joy, peace, and a sound mind for every patient whom I render anesthesia.

Oh, the gentle, soft, calming touch of God makes everything all right. As I tiptoe throughout this earth, I know God has a plan for all of us, a place for us to go – which is Heaven. Prayer changes things – if I have nothing to say, I say, "Jesus." Jesus keeps me balanced and not afraid of facing a trial or new task. He fills any void in my life.

Jesus is my Light and Salvation. The light of a candle represents: life, joy, and peace. Jesus came into the world to bring salvation, joy, and redemption from our sins. The Light shown by Jesus illuminates from my innermost spirit and transmigrates to the surface in my life. Living a holy life is more important than what people think about me. Knowing Jesus paid it all for me. This awareness comes from meditating on the Word of God.

The tribulations and challenges in my life have been overcame one by one by God's Amazing Grace. The pebbles and rocks of life are broken down and made smooth as sand to advance the Word of God. The unconditional love of God is eternal and does not change or falter. He is the same today, tomorrow and forever. I show love to everyone I meet.

Life is a joy when I display love, and look around and see the beauty of this world. Life is peaceful when I rest in God's arms. Dew drops glisten for a moment, then vanish with the return of the sun. My last exhalation and inhalation of air is unknown to me. My life is in God's hand. God is always in control and everything will work out for His Glory and Honor.

I can tell this story of the grieving process through the eyes of a sister and an anesthesiologist because it came to me. I wallowed in it, but I came out of it. God comforted my family and me. He will do it for others. My testimony of passing through this difficult time will assist in drying tears or resolving lonely feelings of others. The calm breeze of the wind on a celestial night becomes a daily walk with God as a Captain of my life. When the turbulent waters come, He is always with me. My glasses may become foggy, but God's knows the direction of my every move. I depend and trust Him to lead me in a serene, crystal clear pathway towards His plan.

Look up, look down, look right and look left. WOW, how wonderful and precious is the sight. If you are experiencing a loss, coping with it is a step-by-step process. We are our brothers' keeper. Offer a helping hand which provides solace to others, then our living will and shall not be in vain. So be it.

~About the Author~

    Renee' Sunday, M.D. is the founder and CEO of Sunday Publishing Company, LLC., and RS Commerce, P.C.

"I have practiced anesthesia for over thirteen years. My mission is to encourage and empower others to enjoy life and obtain their dreams. Furthermore, I enjoy being an instrument in God's Plan to render anesthesia services to my patients and to show compassion, love, and the highest standard of care."

    Renee' is a speaker, mentor, published author and corporate leader. Renee's passion is to be a catalyst to stimulate others forward toward their destiny. She resides in Atlanta, Georgia.

    "God has blessed me with a loving family and friends."

To order additional copies of *Sunday Grief, M.D.,* or to order your *Sunday Comfort Cards* please visit our website at the contact link below.

The *Sunday Comfort Cards* are a resourceful tool to assist in the journey through the grieving process. The *Sunday Comfort Cards* have scripture on one side and a statement of what God said we as believers possess in the particular passage. The cards can be a quick reference of God's Word, which will empower, increase faith, and give strength to transition forward through the grieving process.

Contact e-mail Address:
sundaypublishingcompany@gmail.com

Order your *Sunday Comfort Cards* by visiting:

www.SundayPublishingCompany.com

Sunday Publishing Company
~Journal~

www.ingramcontent.com/pod-product-compliance
Lightning Source LLC
Chambersburg PA
CBHW061651040426
42446CB00010B/1692